SELF-CARE: LOVE YOURSELF

HOW TO EMBRACE SELF-COMPASSION, BODY LOVE & SELF LOVE FOR LIFE-CHANGING WELLNESS & SELF-ESTEEM

ASTON SANDERSON

WALNUT PUBLISHING

CONTENTS

INTRODUCTION

Dear Reader,

Welcome to *Self-Care*, a short guide that will help you live your best life through taking care of the most important person in your life: YOU.

The subtitle for this book is, *How to Embrace Self-Compassion, Body Love and Self Love for Life-Changing Wellness and Self-Esteem.* This subtitle means that we'll be exploring a few different ideas of just what self-care can be. Self-care can mean a lot of different things to different people, and this book will offer you insight into a few different methods of applying self-care:

- **Self-Compassion:** This means feeling an empathy and sympathy toward yourself. This is self-care through **emotions and the spiritual.**
- **Body Love:** This means taking care of yourself **physically.** Often, when we are being self-destructive in our lives, the first thing to go is our physical health, whether that means not exercising, eating junk foods, or not taking time to chill out and relax physically.

- **Self-Love:** In this category, we group together several more kinds of self-care: in the **mental and social** realms.

What does "Life-Changing Wellness and Self-Esteem" mean? This means that when you put the exercises and theories in this book into practice, you will experience a transformation in your life.

A word of caution, though: often, in our present-day society, transformation is sold as a quick-fix. It's just something you can capture in a bottle and buy over-the-counter. All you need is to read one book, or take one course, and voilà! All your dreams have come true. Unfortunately, that's not how real life works.

So, in this book, I'm not telling you that all you need to do is read this short guide, and overnight you'll be a new you. Applying the concepts in this book will be challenging at first. You are taking the first step on a long journey, and I'm not promising it will be easy. But, if you do put in the work, you'll find that the rewards are ten-fold. This is some of the most important work you can do for yourself, for those around you, and for the world. Yes, taking care of yourself is *generous,* not *selfish*. This will be an important point we'll explore further in this book.

If you've found this book, you may be feeling stressed, over-whelmed, exhausted, and frustrated. Maybe you don't know what to do to solve your problems. Maybe you're not sleeping at night, you constantly feel anxious, or you're running around like a chicken with its head cut off.

Take a deep breath.

We'll get through this together.

This guide will help you fight those feelings and replace them with more positive ones. Follow this guide, and you'll be thankful you did.

I'd like to point out that this book is **quite short.** If you want a 300-page book, by all means, find one! But I haven't stuffed this book with filler. *Self-care* gets straight to the point, because I respect your time. I know you're stressed and really feeling that stress, otherwise you wouldn't have made it this far into the introduction! (Or, maybe you are feeling OK, but just want to feel even better. I welcome those readers, too. You'll also find this book helpful.)

So, I've made this book as short and jam-packed as possible. I hope you enjoy that and get a feeling of satisfaction from being able to finish reading it quickly.

There are **end-of-chapter activities** for each section of this book. You may want to move on to a new chapter only after completing the activity, or you may decide that you want to read the entire book and then come back and pick and choose which activities to do, and in what order. Either method is fine, but I do encourage you to walk away from this book having **completed at least one activity** from it.

If you can implement just one practical change in your life from this book, my job will have been complete. Of course, I hope this book I've worked so hard to put together for you accomplishes much more than just one change for you. Readers of my previous books, like *Small Talk* and *Self Talk* have written me to say the books have changed their lives, and they've revisited the books as reference guides many times. I hope you will be able to say the same.

Lastly, I'd like to point out that I am not a medical professional, and the advice in this book does not stand in for medical advice, should you need it. If you are feeling clinically depressed, or in a bad mental state which you're finding hard to climb out of yourself, please contact someone to help you. Maybe ask a friend for help first, if you're afraid of seeking out a mental health professional on your own.

OK, now that you have an introduction to the concept of self-care and what this book will hopefully teach you, let's get started. In the first chapter, we'll discuss what exactly self-care is, in our definition.

Are you ready? Let's dive in!

— Aston Sanderson, Author

1

WHAT IS SELF-CARE?

W hat is "self-care"?

Maybe self-care seems vague and impractical. We've all heard the term "self-care" before, but if you're like most people, you may have never had it defined for you.

In this first chapter, we'll define exactly what self-care means as we use it in this book.

It turns out self-care can mean many different things, but to me, that isn't a negative. That just means that there are many different facets of self-care to explore, and whichever ones resonate with you most are the ones you can adopt for yourself.

Let's dive in to some important aspects of self-care:

A BASIC DEFINITION

A basic definition of self-care is that it's anything you do—mentally or physically—to be kind or nurturing to yourself. That's anything from watching Netflix to unwind (though we'll explore that more deeply in the chapter "Getting Unplugged"), to taking a walk, to repeating an affirmation, such as, "I am a good person" in your mind.

Let's explore some more facets of self-care below.

Self-Care is **Under Your Control**

OK, you're thinking, this is SO obvious. But this aspect of self-care is crucial and cannot be glossed over.

A very important aspect of approaching your self-care journey is having a Growth Mindset instead of a Fixed Mindset. A growth mindset means you believe it is possible to grow and change. A fixed mindset means you believe there are things about yourself that are just black-and-white true.

Let's look at some examples:

Fixed Mindset: "I am bad at learning languages."

Growth Mindset: "I can improve at learning new languages if I put in the work."

Although you started with a rigid idea about yourself that limited your options (you wouldn't even try learning Italian), when you changed your mindset, you suddenly opened a *whole new world of possibilities* for yourself—a new world where you could learn Italian, if you tried.

So how does this relate to self-care? You may have some fixed mindset ideas about self-care, like:

"I just don't have time to take care of myself."

"There are more important things in my life to worry about than me."

"I'm bad at relaxing."

Growth mindset ideas allow for change:

"I can find the time to take care of myself if I get creative with my time management."

"I can learn how to take care of other important things in my life by taking care of me."

"I can learn how to relax better."

So, remember: self-care is under your control.

The biggest block to taking care of yourself isn't your time, or your money, or your prior commitments: it's YOU.

The first step to self-care is believing it's possible to change, to do the work of self-care, to feel better. Take control of your self-care mindset, and you'll be amazed by the things you can achieve.

Self-Care is **Preventative**

Self-care isn't just for de-stressing after a tough day at the office. It isn't only about reacting to stress or negative feelings after they happen, but taking the time to prevent those negative feelings in the first place.

For example, let's say you have a big presentation coming up at work. You could give in to your stressed-out, I'm-freaking-out, nervous feelings in the weeks leading up the presentation, and then book a mini vacation for yourself the weekend after it's done.

But you know what might be better? Booking that weekend getaway the weekend before the presentation. I know, that sounds absolutely crazy. How could you ever find the time? But, if you know you have a small no-work vacation planned, you'll actually find the time to meet your goals ahead of time. Have you ever heard the principle, "Work expands to fill the time allowed for it"? You can do the same amount of work on the presentation—in less time.

And then, when you do take the weekend away right before the presentation, you'll be able to ground yourself. Connect with yourself and who you are away from all the craziness of your job (which, by the way, is not WHO you are!). Allowing for this grounding and connection will give you the perspective to realize your presentation is not The Most Important Thing in the World (which will calm your nerves). In the end it will help you to perform *better* on your presentation.

Pretty wild concept, huh? So, remember that self-care is preventative.

Self-Care is **Restorative**

OK, yes, I will admit, self-care is also restorative. Life, of course, is not predictable. It moves along in ways we never could have expected, and sometimes we'll wake up and realize we are stressed, overwhelmed and stretched too thin, and we have no idea how we got there.

That's perfectly fine, and normal. It happens to all of us more often than we'd like. Even the most preventative self-care can't always take the unknown into account.

So, yes, sometimes self-care means you had the crummiest week and you just need to don sweatpants, get your favorite comfort food and cry. This is a cliché move, but this can be a form of self-care. There may be some reasons you'd be better off putting on real pants, eating a healthy meal, and, OK, maybe still crying at some point. But we'll discuss that in later chapters.

Self-Care is Deliberate

Self-care isn't accidental. You can't say that you'll just make sure to be nice to yourself this week and then expect it to happen. You have to think it through: what will you do for self-care? Why? And then you need to schedule it in and actually do it.

A lot of things you do already in your life may be forms of self-care. Things like meeting up with a good friend, treating yourself to a new gadget or ice cream cone occasionally, journaling, or listening to music. You may not recognize them as self-care right now, and that's fine. Part of reading this book means discovering your self-care plan and what self-care means to you, and then being purposeful about self-care in your life.

Even if you read this book and realize you're doing a spectacular job with self-care, you'll at least be more aware of it and thoughtful about it after going through this guide.

Self-Care is Self-Initiated and Directed

Well, it has "self" in the title, doesn't it? Here's another definition that may seem a bit obvious. This goes hand-in-hand with self-care being a deliberate practice you put into place.

Though it would be nice, we can't outsource the responsibility of self-care to someone else. Even if you're doing well enough financially to have your assistant book you in a weekly massage, you still need to decide if that is the best form of self-care for you. (Because as you'll learn in later chapters, what we often think of as relaxation— the aforementioned sweatpants, a massage—are actually not super helpful for taking care of ourselves.)

So, self-care is *your* job. But this is actually quite freeing. You don't need to call a meeting. You don't need to check with others. (OK, maybe your spouse or partner if it means rescheduling something for the family so you can get some alone time.) But you are the boss here. And if you need some time away, hopefully the people in your life understand you're doing what's best for you and will accommodate you.

SELF-CARE IS MEDICINAL, Spiritual, Mental, Physical and Philosophical

Self-care, in medical terms, might mean putting a Band-Aid on a cut yourself, without a medical professional's help. In philosophy, self-care might mean coming to an understanding of a greater sense of self.

In this book, self-care has many different facets: spiritual, emotional, physical, mental, and yes, medicinal and philosophical, too.

We'll go more into these types of self-care in the next chapter, but for now, just know that whatever specific area of your life in which you need self-care right now, that's the area you can focus on as you go through this book.

WHAT ISN'T SELF-CARE?

Self-care *isn't* selfish. We'll have a whole chapter explaining why that's true later on in this book. But when you take care of yourself, that actually means you'll have greater energy and emotional and mental capacity to care for others. So if you want to help others, help yourself first.

Self-care also isn't *indulgent.* People may think taking time for themselves is a waste of time or energy, but it is necessary. Everyone needs some time that's just for them. After all, relationships, jobs, homes, etc. will all come and go throughout the course of your life, but you'll have a relationship with yourself from Day 1 until the end. So you better make sure it's a good one!

We've gone over a few definitions and important aspects of self-care in this chapter, so you should have a greater idea of what you're getting into, what self-care means in general, and which aspects of self-care resonate most with you.

IN THE NEXT CHAPTER, we'll dive deeper into the different types of self-care, drilling down from vague ideas about the topic and getting more practical and literal for your everyday life.

ACTIVITY

For this chapter, your activity will be very easy, to get you on a roll with the other end-of-chapter activities. For this activity, choose which attribute of self-care with which you most identify. For example, choose a bolded subject heading like "Self-Care is Deliberate" or "Self-Care is Self-Initiated."

Write this definition on a post-it note, scrap piece of paper, old receipt, whatever! And use this as your bookmark for your book. If you're reading on a Kindle or e-reader (or your phone), put the note in a place where you are likely to see it each day. Maybe this is your bedroom nightstand or your bathroom mirror. Just put it somewhere where you will be reminded of this aspect of self-care that most appeals to you.

This activity will urge you to spend more time thinking about self-care. And when you have an easy definition of one aspect of self-care to remember, it will stick in your head. So, take 30 seconds to scratch out this message and put it somewhere to help keep self-care forefront in your mind.

2

TYPES OF SELF-CARE

In this chapter, we'll delve into different kinds of self-care. Self-care activities can fall into different types, and you may find that certain categories resonate more with you than others. That's OK. Trying to focus on all of them at once, and going from 'zero-to-60' may leave you feeling more burned out than when you started! And that's the opposite of self-care. So, for now, just see which ones spark a bit of interest for you, or which categories you know you need to work on in your own self-care.

Let's look at the self-care categories.

EMOTIONAL

Self-care that is emotion-based is focused on your feelings. Sometimes we can let our emotions overwhelm us and drive us. But focusing too much on controlling your emotions with an iron fist is also a recipe for disaster. A happy medium or balance with your emotions is key.

When you do emotional self-care, this is anything that puts you in touch with your inner emotions more deeply, or that affects your mood. Examples of emotional self-care are journaling about your feelings, writing thank you notes to connect more deeply with grati-tude, or having a good cry if you need it.

SENSORY

Sensory self-care is about being mindful and connecting more deeply with your surroundings. These self-care activities will relate to the five senses: touch, taste, sight, smell and sound. This may mean eating a favorite chocolate to delight in the sense of rich taste, going on a walk in nature to pay attention to the light cascading through the trees or the sounds of the birds, or simply lighting your favorite-smelling candle and taking in the aroma.

This type of self-care can be very helpful for brining you back to the present moment. Often, when we're overwhelmed and stressed, our thoughts swirl around our brain at a rapid pace and we can't seem to get control or slow them down.

Sensory self-care brings us back into our body and slows our thoughts by slowing our awareness. When you are focusing on the smell of your favorite candle, it is much harder to think about every-thing you need to do next week.

PHYSICAL

Physical self-care can be related to sensory self-care, as they both focus on the body. But whereas sensory self-care focuses on the five senses, physical self-care is more about body love, or treating our bodies as temples, as the saying goes. Examples of physical self-care could be getting a massage, going for a run, stretching or doing yoga, or having a soothing bubble bath.

This type of self-care helps us to ground ourselves in the present moment by paying attention to our bodies and showing love for them. Sometimes we believe our bodies are separate from our minds, but everything is interconnected. Why do we get sick when we are feeling stressed? Why do we feel like we have tons of energy when we're excited about something, even if we didn't sleep very much last night? It's because of the mind-body connection. Our minds and bodies are interlinked more than we know, and the simple act of caring for your body has a calming effect on the mind.

This is a very gentle and loving form of self-care, but one with which people sometimes struggle. They might not feel they deserve to treat their bodies well, but that is a topic we'll discuss in a further chapter.

SPIRITUAL

Spiritual self-care relates to emotional self-care, but expands our area of focus from the self and the emotions to the whole world, the universe, and higher beings. Whether you follow a specific religion or not, spiritual self-care is important. Examples of this activity could be praying, meditating, or visiting a religious service or monument. No matter what specifically makes you feel spiritual and connected to a powerful force outside yourself, taking the time to identify something meaningful to you will bring huge dividends.

Finding our place in this world and having perspective is a great force for self-care.

SOCIAL

Social self-care is one of my personal favorites. Often, when I'm feeling in a rut, the last thing I want to do is go out and see people. But afterward, I always feel a thousand times better than before. Even if I dread it, a social situation forces me to share a bit of myself with people and to receive their contribution to our relationship back.

Social doesn't have to mean attending a giant party. It could just be calling, emailing, or texting a friend. Though nothing can replace in-person communication and togetherness, sometimes we just need to know there's someone else out there who cares about us.

MENTAL

The last form of self-care is mental self-care. This means finding something to challenge your brain and stoke your curiosity. Examples of mental self-care are doing the crossword, reading a book, or taking a cooking class to learn something new.

Mental self-care is great for us because when we are focusing on learning a new skill or concentrating on solving a puzzle, this takes over our working memory, and we can no longer focus on how down we are feeling. Finishing a sudoku puzzle or a book also gives us a great feeling of having done something productive.

These are the different types of self-care: emotional, sensory, physical, spiritual, social, and mental. You should now have a better understanding of what each of these types of self-care mean, and so in the next chapter, we'll delve into a huge list of examples of each.

ACTIVITY

The activity for this chapter is to identify which area of self-care most appeals to you. Though drawing from each category at different times makes for a well-rounded self-care routine, for now, don't bite off more than you can chew—just focus on one area that appeals to you.

Free-write about why this category appeals to you. It can be just one sentence, or maybe you end up writing a full page. Don't judge what you write; just let your thoughts flow directly onto the page. You won't show anyone this. It's just for you.

For example, maybe mental self-care appeals to you because you love puzzles. Write about the first time you remember enjoying a puzzle as a child. Maybe social self-care appeals to you because you feel disconnected from your friends. Write about what those relationships mean to you. Maybe physical self-care appeals to you because you miss hiking. Write about what your body feels like before, during and after a hike.

3

LIST OF SELF-CARE IDEAS & ACTIVITIES

I n this chapter, you'll find a huge list of self-care activities to get the wheels turning in your brain. Of course, this is not an exhaustive list. You can be creative and come up with your own self-care activities.

Sometimes when we are stressed, just the idea of having to decide what to do overwhelms us. You should have a go-to self-care activities list to take the stress out of having to decide and brainstorm. Just taking the first step is often the hardest part, but once we sit down to write, or put on our running shoes, the rest just flows from there.

So, this list is to help you take that first step. Some of these activities could fall into multiples categories at once, or into different categories based on how you approach them. For example, a hike in nature could be emotional, spiritual, sensory or physical. I've just included each activity once and separated them as best as I can, but know that the categories are not rigid.

Also, some activities may be things you can accomplish in just a few minutes (spend time in the sun), while others are lasting activities that become a regular routine (join a new club.)

.   .   .

ACTIVITY

For this chapter, I'll let you know a bit about the activity before we start. Get a scrap piece of paper (or open a note on your phone) and write down the self-care activities that immediately jump out to you as something you'd like to do.

EMOTIONAL SELF-CARE ACTIVITIES

- Journaling
- Crying
- Laughing
- See a therapist
- Declutter: clean a room or just one drawer
- Help someone with a small act of kindness
- Ask for help from someone else
- Unplug from your devices for an hour
- Play! Be goofy or silly
- Make a list of compliments people have given you in the past, or reach out and ask for new ones

SENSORY SELF-CARE ACTIVITIES

- Listen to music
- Sing along to music
- Eat a favorite food
- Snuggle up under a soft blanket
- Meditate
- Light a candle
- Pet an animal
- Take a warm bath
- Walk barefoot outside or lay in the grass (grounding)
- Spend time in nature

- Take photographs
- Get fresh air
- Spend time in the sun
- Take deep breaths

PHYSICAL SELF-CARE ACTIVITIES

- Yoga
- Stretching
- Dancing
- Hiking
- Going for a walk
- Going for a run
- Getting a massage
- Taking a nap
- Playing a team sport
- Swimming
- Painting your nails, doing a face mask or get a haircut

SPIRITUAL SELF-CARE ACTIVITIES

- Attend a religious service
- Visit a religious monument or building
- Pray
- Meditate
- Read poetry or spiritual texts
- Just sit still and be for 10 minutes

SOCIAL SELF-CARE ACTIVITIES

- Call a good friend
- Write a letter to someone
- Attend a party or social gathering
- Message a friend
- Re-connect with someone you haven't spoken to in a while
- Join a club of some kind
- Join a support group of some kind
- Put an end to a relationship that is toxic

MENTAL SELF-CARE ACTIVITIES

- Do a crossword or sudoku
- Do a jigsaw puzzle
- Read a book
- Listen to a podcast or radio show
- Visit the library
- Take up a new skill or hobby
- Take a class in an area that interests you
- Read about a topic you've never learned about before
- Drive somewhere new or take a new route home from work
- Do a craft project
- Do something that takes you out of your comfort zone

ACTIVITY

OK, now that you have a list written down of activities that appeal to you, this chapter activity should be easy! Or at least, the first part is: pick ONE, yes, ONE activity from the list in this chapter.

Here's the hard part: schedule it into your calendar in the next week. Yes, you can find the time!

Here's the even harder part: when the day comes around for your self-care activity, you're NOT ALLOWED to cancel or reschedule it. Pretend this is an important meeting with your boss. No, wait, pretend it's your boss's boss. Or your favorite celebrity. Whatever works for you! But pretend this is with someone *so* important that you simply *cannot* not do it, no matter an earthquake, a traffic jam, a sickness, or, well, the feeling that you just don't want to do it.

Remember: this meeting, after all, *is* with the most important person you shouldn't cancel on: yourself.

4

THE BENEFITS OF SELF-CARE

In this chapter, I'm going to tell you why we are setting out on this self-care journey together. You've found your way to this book, so you already have an interest in what self-care can do for you. But I think the benefits are even more profound than you may think.

Self-care all comes back to our view of our own self-worth. Often, we say we're not taking care of ourselves because we're too busy or stressed or have other obligations. These are just surface-level reasons. The true reason we are not finding time for self-care is because, deep-down, we feel we don't deserve it.

When we start to take care of ourselves more seriously, we start to love ourselves more. Just by caring for ourselves, we can boost our own self-esteem. Beliefs come from actions, not the other way around. You don't need to believe you are worth a spa day to make it happen. But once you make it happen, you begin to believe it.

Another example: maybe you don't believe meditating for 15 minutes every day will have any benefits to your life. That's fine. Do it anyway, if it's your chosen self-care activity. When you start to meditate for 15 minutes every day, you'll start to have a calmer mind, a more present and focused awareness, and a less reactive emotional balance in your life. Then you start to believe that meditation can bring benefits to your belief.

They say seeing is believing, but I say *doing is believing.*

So, when you start to care for yourself with the self-care activities and routines listed in this book, you start to raise your own self-esteem. When you start to care for your body as if it is precious (and isn't it? Without it, you'd be...nothing!), you start to believe that it is. Maybe you don't feel a lot of love toward your body now, but when you start to treat your body nicely, you begin to believe it is worthy and beautiful.

This is an especially short chapter because the activity in it is very important, so I want you to have plenty of time to explore it.

ACTIVITY

Think of an important relationship in your life, someone who loves you. Think of how that person treats you. Most likely with kindness, compassion, forgiveness. Think of the love that person feels for you. Think about how it makes you feel to receive that love. How does it make you feel to know that this person is always there for you? How do you feel in response to this person, in knowing how they feel about you?

Either think about these topics, or do some free-writing on them for as long as you wish. Have a specific person in mind, and be as specific as you can. Was there a specific thing they did for you that was kind? Something they said to you that sticks in your mind? Either an affirmation of their love, of your relationship, or a compliment?

Now, for the next part of this exercise, I want you to write about yourself in the same way. Maybe you don't feel very kind to yourself at the moment, or you don't feel a lot of self-love. That's OK. Write about what is possible. How would you feel if you felt true love from yourself? Would it feel similar to the love you feel from that other person you wrote about in the first part of this exercise?

What could you achieve in your life that you've been hiding from or putting off because you aren't kind enough to yourself or can't forgive yourself?

Think of the benefits of having a relationship with yourself that is as deep and loving as that of a friend, romantic partner or family member. Go as deep as you can with this activity to see the most benefit.

5

SELF-CARE IS A HABIT

In this chapter, I'm going to focus on incorporating self-care into your daily life.

Self-care would be easy if it just meant that every time we felt like we needed a break, we could schedule a week holiday and treat ourselves with an all-inclusive resort. Unfortunately, that's rarely the reality because of our over-packed schedules, our commitments, our budgets, and what actually makes us feel good.

You can't take a sabbatical from your life whenever you feel like you need some me-time. You have to incorporate self-care into your life. You have to make the space each and every day—yes, everyday! —to give yourself more compassion.

On a daily basis we often rush through life, going from task to task, and we forget to check in with ourselves. If we leave our decompression until we get home at the end of the day, we're already stressed and exhausted. A much better method is to decompress throughout the day instead of just at the end.

For example, just checking in with how you are feeling is one of the easiest and best forms of self-care you can do—just being aware of yourself and being present. Fortunately, this is a form of self-care that is easy to incorporate into your daily routine.

Set a reminder on your phone for once or twice throughout the day. When this reminder comes up, no matter what you are doing, you can take five deep breaths. Feel your feet on the floor and the sensory experience of the room. Identify how you are feeling physically, emotionally and mentally in that moment. Sometimes just naming how we are feeling helps us gain some distance from it.

Or maybe you build a self-care habit. Maybe you spend the last five minutes of lunch journaling, or you wake up 15 minutes earlier to be the first one up and enjoy your coffee as you look out the window —not racing to get ready or looking at your phone, but just sitting in silence and appreciating.

Another way to incorporate self-care into your daily routine is to make it a habit or take up a recurring activity. Maybe you've always wanted to learn how to knit or to roller skate. Join a local club, class or team and then stick to the schedule. It will be something you look forward to all week, and therefore something that has lasting benefits outside of just the hour you have to practice per week.

Self-care should be activities that you want to do. They are mini-indulgences. Often, we spend so much of our lives doing what we feel we should do, or what we feel we have to do. Self-care activities are those that you want to do. They don't need to have a purpose; they can be silly or random or "pointless." The whole point is to do something just for you.

Be aware as well that sometimes self-care activities, if they are new hobbies or passions, can become just another thing you have to do. Let's say you take up roller skating at the local rink, and then you join the roller dance team, and then you have another obligation. Try to remember why it is you started your self-care activity, instead of making it just another item on your to-do list for the day.

Building self-care as a habit is the important part. On good days when you are feeling great and energized and motivated, doing a small self-care activity will be easy. It's the days when you are feeling stressed, busy and tired that making the effort for self-care will be hard. So, this is the most important time to do self-care. Remember, self-care doesn't have to be huge: it can be taking a 20-

minute rest, watching a funny video on YouTube, or just taking five deep breaths.

But when you make self-care into a habit, you make it a part of your life, and that's the important part. Self-care is daily, not a once-in-a-blue-moon treat.

Treat yourself every day; you deserve it.

ACTIVITY

Pick a self-care activity that takes less than five minutes to do. Over the next week, try to do this activity every day. They say it takes 21 days to build a habit, so aiming for three weeks is even better. But for now, start small.

6

SELF-CARE IS A LIFESTYLE

Self-care is not only a daily habit, but a lifestyle. What do I mean by lifestyle? I mean the overarching way you live your life.

Sometimes we let healthy ways of life slip. When we have a family that needs taking care of, or a big project at work that needs all our focus, we forget to pay any attention to how we are living our lives. How much sleep are you getting? How often are you eating foods that fuel your body and mind in healthy ways? How often are you getting outside? Or doing a little exercise? Are you taking care of your mental health?

In popular culture, the idea of self-care might mean tucking in for four hours of Netflix with a big tub of ice cream. While a bit of indulgent self-care can be OK sometimes, real and lasting self-care is the kind that really makes you feel good, inside and out.

Netflix and ice cream is a temporary fix. It's like a Band-Aid. Sometimes we do have just a little cut, and the Band-Aid will help. But sometimes, our wrist is sprained or our arm is broken, and a Band-Aid just won't do.

So, self-care is a healthy lifestyle. True self-care means doing things for yourself that help you feel better for longer than the activity lasts. Self-care has lasting mental, physical, emotional, spiritual and social benefits. They are activities that truly feed your soul, not just your surface cravings.

Eating healthy and getting some exercise may be the last things you want to do to take care of yourself when you're feeling down, but these are the activities that will make you feel good for hours and days afterward. This contrasts with the TV and ice cream, which will make you feel good in the moment, but may make you feel guilty, bloated and regretful once they end.

When you are evaluating self-care activities, ask yourself how long the benefits will last. Is this an activity that will make you feel good while it's happening, but even worse afterwards? Or is it something that will nourish you in a deep and lasting way?

So, evaluate activities: is this chocolate a tiny indulgence that I will appreciate? Or a double-serving that will make me sick? Is this friend someone who supports me, or someone who always tends to bring me down? Yes, even in social settings, we can have people in our lives that aren't good for us, but we continue the relationships for whatever reason. Don't let any activity go without scrutiny.

Overall, self-care is about being kind to yourself. And being kind to yourself in the long-term sometimes means kicking your own butt into gear to get off the couch and go for a walk, breathing that fresh air and seeing some sunshine, even if you don't want to in the moment. In a way, self-care sometimes means being a bit tough with yourself.

Often, we're in a place where we're in dire need of self-care because we've let our immediate indulgences, cravings, and knee-jerk emotional reactions get the best of us. Self-care doesn't mean giving in to these. It means taking the time to figure out what really makes you happy and feel cared for in a lasting way.

This is not always easy to figure out, but with this book, it is a journey that is worth going on, and one we'll help you with.

GETTING Unplugged

Now I want to mention an aspect of self-care that may be left out of many discussions of the topic.

In this day and age, I want you to pay special attention to self-care in relation to digital devices and being 'connected' all the time. Being connected to the world, the news, work, friends and messages 24 hours a day, seven days a week is enough to leave anyone drained, morose and overwhelmed.

While connection can be self-care in itself, not all connection is good. And it is easy to be over-connected in our current society. Let's take a minute to focus on how unplugging on a daily basis or taking sabbaticals from our devices can be a form of self-care.

When we think of a healthy lifestyle, we think of exercising and eating right. But one very important form of health is getting away from screens and devices. Connecting with nature, with ourselves and with our bodies is so important for feeling grounded, present and healthy.

Though it may be hard at first to put down your phone, tablet or take a break from the TV, doing so will ultimately help you connect with yourself.

Easy ways to go without your devices is to take a walk without your phone, or eat a meal without your phone nearby. Allow yourself to be bored. Allow your mind and thoughts to wander. Being bored is healthy for us. We don't need constant stimulation. Remember that unplugging—just for 20 minutes or for an entire weekend—can be a self-care activity.

ACTIVITY

Look at the habit self-care activity you chose in the last chapter, and the self-care activity you chose from the list of activities chapter. Evaluate these activities. Do they make you feel good in the short-term, medium-term, or long-term? Are they nourishing and healthy, or indulgent? If they are not the best lifestyle self-care activities, is there a way to make them healthier? If not, consider swapping out for a healthier self-care activity.

7

SELF-CARE IS KNOWING YOURSELF

Self-care is all about YOU. And that means knowing yourself. How can we care for ourselves if we don't know ourselves? It may seem like knowing yourself would be something you wouldn't even have to think about. After all, you spend every waking moment with yourself. How would you not know yourself best?

But often, our ideas about who we are or what we truly like are skewed. They're influenced by who we want to be or wish we were, our society and culture, our family and friends, our work environment, and our pasts. Each of us is complicated and full of contradictions. We may love meeting up with friends one night, and the next night, relish our time alone. Sometimes alone time makes us feel lonely. Sometimes social activities make us feel lonely. We can have one persona in one situation, and act differently in another. Who we are is constantly evolving, but are we in tune with these subtle shifts?

If you've chosen a self-care activity of joining a recreational softball team again because you loved it when you played 10 years ago, will you still love it? Maybe you will reconnect with a sport that you truly found joy in back then, and you'll still love it now. But maybe you've grown into someone who doesn't really get enjoyment out of softball anymore, and that's OK, too. Our interests and passions change, and sticking to one idea of ourselves is not good for our self-care.

The more you know about yourself, the better you'll be at administering self-care. For example, a lot of people would look at massages as a form of self-care. Personally, I find them a bit boring and awkward. So, if I was trying to force myself to get massages to relax, it's actually doing the opposite and stressing me out. I'd be much better off spending that money and time on something I actually enjoy, instead of something I feel I'm supposed to enjoy. Maybe a computer programming course, which would be a mental form of self-care.

Paying attention to what you actually like and makes you feel good is important in self-care. You're the only one you need to please here. Don't worry about whether you're doing self-care "right" or the "correct" way. The most correct way is getting the most out of it that you can.

A form of self-care is spending time getting to know yourself. Noticing what gives you energy and makes you excited versus what drains you is essential to understanding yourself.

Personality tests are one way that you can learn more about yourself. You can often find free assessments online to help you learn about your personality. Some of the most famous personality tests are:

- Enneagram
- Myers-Briggs
- StrengthsFinder

THERE ARE LOTS MORE. What matters isn't that you pick the right test, but what you decide to find meaning in with the results. If the test tells you that you would love analytical forms of work like math and spreadsheets, but you know you love writing, you have the ultimate say. Don't follow what the personality test says as the law.

The tests are just a means to get you to be more self-reflective. Maybe you have never considered yourself an analytical person before, but now that you think about it, maybe you *are*. Maybe more math-focused work would benefit you. The personality test results are a catalyst for thinking about yourself in new ways.

Read the descriptions of the personality type the results give you, and see what sticks out to you. Taking the time to get to know ourselves and who we truly are is one of the best forms of self-care.

ACTIVITY

TAKE one of the personality tests listed (or find another one you want to try). Read the results and see if you've learned anything new about yourself. How can you apply something you've learned to your self-care activities?

8

SELF-CARE IS NOT SELFISH

Now that we're this far into our discussion of self-care, I think it's time to point out something very important: self-care is NOT selfish.

People make excuses for not taking care of themselves that sound very altruistic and legitimate. "I have too many family obligations." "I have too many work obligations." "Other people need me too much."

While all these things may be true, you can't take care of someone else before you take care of yourself. By replenishing your own stores of energy and self-love, you are then free to give your energy and love to others.

Self-care can sound indulgent. Why would you spend all that money and time on yourself, when there are other more practical uses for them? But self-care is about allowing yourself to play, to feel freer, to feel more in control of yourself and of your life.

Even if you set aside just $5 a month as your "play money" for self-care, you can spend it on something truly enjoyable. A new set of colored pencils for your adult coloring books. Your favorite chocolate bar. A train ticket to a place near your town that you've never been. The point is that you give yourself license to do something that doesn't have a point or practical purpose, but is just for fun, for play, and for YOU.

Sometimes we believe that we are not deserving of our own love and nurturing. This can be one of the most difficult realities to face in your self-care journey: finding the underlying reason why you're not taking care of yourself. Maybe someone said something hurtful to you when you were young, and you've believed that you're inferior ever since.

Maybe you've had toxic relationships in your life that have left you with low self-confidence. These are harsh roads to explore, but if you do, you'll be healing wounds that only you can heal. If you feel truly overwhelmed and lost, see a mental health professional. Otherwise, do journaling or find books that help you resolve past issues and experiences that are affecting your own view of your self-worth today.

You deserve to enjoy your life.

You deserve kindness, from others and from yourself.

You are worth love.

You are worth compassion, from yourself and from others.

You are worth self-care.

A Self-Care Note for Parents & Caregivers

Here's a very important note about self-care in our current culture. These days there's something online called "Mommy Shaming." This ridiculous practice involves criticizing the way other parents raise their children, usually on a Facebook post or other social media post.

I'm here to say that you shouldn't be afraid of mommy shaming on your self-care journey. Whether you are a parent, grandparent, caregiver or guardian, you have the right to still be your own person. You are in charge of someone else, it's true, but that doesn't mean you stop existing.

Taking time for yourself or doing something that other people might think is selfish does not mean it is. You are the own judge of your life, and an adult. You have the power to assess what you think is right, what you need and what your family needs. As a leader in your family, you need to nurture yourself and your relationships to be able to lead properly.

ACTIVITY

Journal for 5-10 minutes about what you believe you deserve. Then write down what you believe a good friend deserves.

Afterward, read back what you have written. Do you have any limiting beliefs about what you think you deserve? Did you notice you were much kinder to your friend than to yourself? We are usually kinder to others than to ourselves, which, when you think about it, just doesn't make sense. We are our own best friends and should treat ourselves as kindly as we treat others.

9

SELF-CARE STARTS IN YOUR BRAIN

I have written a related book to this one called *Self Talk*, and it is all about how we talk to ourselves in our brain. This is an essential topic to discuss for self-care as well. Even if we go through the motions of being kind to ourselves by joining the local gym, visiting the local spa or catching up with a good friend, we can still be cruel to ourselves with our thought patterns. In this chapter, we'll discuss how to change your negative self-talk to positive self-talk.

We are constantly running unconscious patterns of thought in our heads. And they really are patterns that get stuck in there, like the refrain to a catchy song. They are unconscious, meaning we don't realize we're doing this. We don't realize how harmful it is. They say the average person's inner mental chatter is about 80 percent negative. But the good news is that each of us has the power to change our inner mental chatter. It is as simple as rewiring the patterns and creating new ones. It may not be easy, and it will take some work and time, but it is very much worth it, and your self-care journey will suffer without this important aspect.

Let's discuss a few different types of negative self-talk.

· · ·

THE FIRST TYPE IS FILTERING, which is when we filter out the 10 compliments we received about our new haircut and focus on the one person who didn't seem like they liked it very much. Why not focus on the compliments instead? Our brain is wired to lean toward the negative. Be aware of this.

The second type is **catastrophizing**, which is when we go down a thought spiral of negative thinking. When one bad thing happens, we assume more is to follow, or we think of all the bad things going on in our life. Realize that one bad thought leads to another, and try to stop a negative thought spiral.

The next type of negative self-talk is **personalizing**, which is when we assume that bad things that happen are directed specifically at us, instead of realizing that bad things happen all the time, and we shouldn't take them as personal attacks.

Polarizing is when we see things as black and white, good and bad, with no room for considering the silver lining, the blessing in disguise, or that most things in life are gray, neither good nor bad but somewhere in-between. It's up to us which side we focus on.

Rehashing is dwelling on the past and getting caught up in what we should have done or should have said. Be kind to yourself by forgiving yourself for things you feel you've done wrong in the past. Dwelling on them doesn't help and only makes you feel bad about yourself. See what you can learn to do differently next time and move on.

Rehearsing is worrying about the future. You may imagine all the negative ways your work presentation can go, trying to prepare for each one. Instead, focus on how your presentation will go right, and take some of the stress off of yourself.

And finally, the last type of negative self-talk is **blaming**, which is when we take on other peoples' problems or bad days and find a way to make them our fault. Everyone is responsible for their own reactions and dispositions. Don't blame yourself for someone else's problems. Caring about another person is different than blaming yourself.

. . .

NOW THAT WE'VE covered a few types of negative self-talk, you'll be more aware of how you use these types in your own head. Just being able to recognize a type of negative self-talk helps you get some distance from it. Remember that you are not your thoughts. You have the power to change them.

Now let's look at some strategies for changing your negative self-talk into positive, self-caring thoughts.

1. **Recognize your inner critic.** One way to get some distance from the critical voice in your head is to give it a name. Yes, an actual name. See your negative thoughts as coming from another person, not from within yourself. What would you do if someone in real life was as mean to yourself as you are in your head? You'd hopefully ignore them and realize they are trying to hurt you. So, imagine your negative thoughts are coming from a different person, and dismiss them.

2. **Investigate your thoughts.** Another strategy is to investigate a negative thought when it comes into your head. Ask yourself, where did this thought first come from? Was it something a teacher or parent said to you when you were little? Something you read? Can you identify this thought as one of the seven types of negative self-talk? Ask yourself, is this thought useful? What might a more useful thought be? A more positive thought on this topic? When we question our negative thoughts about ourselves, we realize they often have no basis in reality. Your negative thoughts are guilty of being useless, mean and unfounded in reality until proven innocent. I think you'll find they are usually guilty of all of these traits!

3. **Use affirmations.** It's hard to replace a repetitive negative script when we don't have anything to replace it with. Write down nice things about yourself. If you have trouble, ask friends for compliments, or what your strengths are, or what they admire about you or like best about you. Write down the nice things you'd tell a friend, and then change them from "you" to "I".

·   ·   ·

ACTIVITY

What's something you say to yourself on a regular basis that is not very nice? Investigate this thought, and find a positive thought with which to replace it.

CONCLUSION

Thank you for reading this book on self-care. I hope you have come away from it with at least one change you can make in your life, which will help you to be kinder to yourself and to take better care of your most important relationship.

I hope this book will become a reference for you as you go through your self-care journey. Its short length makes it an easy book to revisit when you are feeling down or stressed. I didn't want to pack this book with lots of fluff, because I believe taking action is more important than hearing the same advice over and over.

The most important part of this book moving forward is that you do take action. If you haven't done any of the end-of-chapter activities yet, go back through the book and pick out one to do in the next day. You may feel resistant to taking action, but the first step is often the hardest. Once you get the ball rolling, you will find that the self-care, self-love and self-compassion you can give will snowball. Each action you take, however small or big, builds on the last, and it will keep building and building.

You will feel greater self-confidence, greater presence and aware-ness in your daily life, and feel more in tune and appreciative of your body.

I have one more end-of-chapter **activity** for you:

Of course, making these changes is not easy. Is there someone in your life you are close enough with to tell them you are embarking on this self-care journey? It might feel scary to open up, but try telling one person what you are trying to accomplish, and ask for their support. Ask them to check in with you later this week and ask if you did the self-care tasks you set out to do.

You will be surprised how supportive this other person will be. Maybe they will even be intrigued by your journey and want to go on it with you. Though self-care is ultimately up to you, having another person going on their own journey, side by side, will help keep both of you accountable.

I am so happy I am able to share the strategies in this book with you, and I truly hope you found them helpful. As an indie author, I depend a lot on reviews for my books, so if you have one minute and something nice to say, please leave me a review. [insert link]

I can also be reached at aston@walnutpub.com if you'd like to reach out individually. Readers of my previous books, *Small Talk, Self Talk* and *Minimalist Living,* have reached out to say the books have changed their lives in small and large ways. This is why I write, for you, my reader.

My books don't connect with everyone, but that's OK. If this book didn't connect with you, I hope you still took away one practical thing. I believe self-care is something we all need more of in our life. Developing the most important relationship in your life—with your-self—is so important for a healthy and happy life, one in which we can give our best selves to other people.

Always remember:

You deserve love and compassion.

You are worth kindness.

You are a good person.

You deserve loving, gentle self-care.

Your Author,
    Aston Sanderson

DID YOU ENJOY THIS BOOK?

I personally read every review my books receive.

I look forward to reading yours.

Please leave a review on Amazon by visiting your recent orders page or searching for the title of this book.

With Gratitude,
Aston Sanderson

ABOUT THE AUTHOR: ASTON SANDERSON

Aston Sanderson is passionate about helping people lead better lives through short, conversational and fun books. He is the author of "Small Talk," a manual for better conversations, "Self Talk," a guide to practicing more self-love, and "Minimalist Living," a helpful way to declutter your life. He loves to hear from readers at aston@walnut-pub.com for book feedback and ideas of what readers want to learn about next. His books are available in many languages worldwide.

Printed in Great Britain
by Amazon